Loch Ness

and Inverness

Photography by Colin Baxter
Text by Julie Davidson

Colin Baxter Photography Ltd, Grantown-on-Spey, Scotland

Beauty and the Beast

The nature of Loch Ness invites mystery. Depths of over 240 m (800 ft) have been plumbed, and the chilling, peat-rich gloom of its waters means that divers and submersibles lose daylight a few metres below the surface. Its steep-sided trench was caused by the movement of tectonic plates during the Ice Age, and it is the largest of the three lochs which, linked by the River Ness, the River Lochy and the Caledonian Canal, can be accessed from both the Atlantic Ocean and the North Sea.

But the worldwide reputation of Loch Ness, which has displaced Loch Lomond as Scotland's most renowned stretch of water, is a recent affair – and owes its celebrity almost exclusively to the legend, lore and scientific enigma of its residential 'monster'. If the search for the Loch Ness Monster has become part of a thriving tourist industry there is, however, much more to explore along the 38 km (24 miles) and steep wooded banks of Britain's greatest volume of fresh water.

Drumnadrochit, whose handsome Victorian fishing hotel now houses the Official Loch Ness Monster Exhibition, is the nerve centre of the Nessie industry. The waters off Urquhart Castle, about 3 km (2 miles) from the village, have produced the greatest number of Nessie sightings, and a small fleet of sonar-equipped motor launches offers scenic cruises – with the added inducement of potentially interesting sonar echoes.

But the village, which owes its existence to an easy crossing of the River Endrick on the route between Inverness and the south-west, has its own charm, and provides various facilities for visitors, including souvenir shops and Nessie memorabilia, as well as places to eat. Unusually for a Scottish settlement it is endowed with a village green, where sheep and cattle were once rested on drives to the market towns.

The road west from Drumnadrochit takes you through Glen Urquhart and past Corrimony Cairn, which is believed to date back to the Bronze Age, and on to Cannich and Glen Affric, one of the finest in Scotland.

However, the splendid setting of Drumnadrochit, at the junction of Glen Urquhart and the Great Glen, is reason enough to linger. Those not exclusively infected with monster fever can enjoy its natural spectacles, some of which have been helped along by human intervention. Abriachan Nurseries, some 0.8 ha (2 acres) of brilliant plants and their

Loch Ness, looking to the north-east.

Loch Ness from the shores of its northern end (opposite). Scotland's most famous stretch of water is offset by the beguiling beauty of its surroundings. Its deep trench was caused by the movement of tectonic plates during the last Ice Age.

Urquhart Castle as it might have appeared in the late 16th century (above). Its ruins today (opposite) date largely from this period, but there has been a castle on this strategic site since the 12th century.

inarguably one of Scotland's most theatrically sited ruins – and the most extensive. In its day the castle was among the largest in Scotland, the successor to an Iron Age fort which once stood on this conspicuously defensive bluff. Strategically important during Scotland's medieval Wars of Independence against England, it was taken and retaken by Edward I of England, who enlarged and strengthened it, and held by Robert the Bruce against Edward III. It passed through several hands until James IV gifted it to John Grant of Freuchie in 1509, and he built most of the structure which remains today.

marketable seedlings, are only 9.5 km (6 miles) up the A82, and a hearty walk from the village brings you to Divach Falls, which with their 30 m (100 ft) drop are among the highest in the Highlands. Neighbouring Divach Lodge was once the rural retreat of Dame Ellen Terry, the distinguished actress. Among the guests she entertained there was J.M. Barrie, the author of *Peter Pan*.

Drumnadrochit's showcase asset, however, is Urquhart Castle, which stands on an eloquent green headland overlooking Urquhart Bay. It is

But the castle didn't merely crumble away through neglect over the intervening centuries. It was reduced to its present state in 1692, when it was blown up to prevent Jacobite revolutionaries making use of it.

Today, its romantic remnants are the subject of some upgrading works nearby, at the entrance to the castle grounds beside the A82, where Historic Scotland, the government-appointed organisation who are the castle's custodians, have built a new visitor centre.

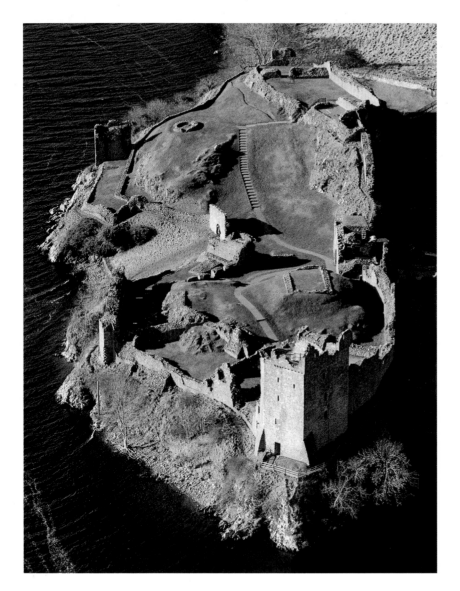

Urquhart Castle, seen here from the air, is one of the most extensive ruined fortifications in Scotland, and also the most visited site on the shores of Loch Ness.

The prodigious volume of water in Loch Ness dominates activities round its shores, and Caledonian Canal cruises, from the Moray Firth to Loch Linnhe at the southern end of the Great Glen, have become fixtures of the leisure industry – for both self-steer sailors, who can charter cabin cruisers from a number of moorings, and those who prefer to be passengers. Only about 35 km (22 miles) of this 96 km (60 mile) channel from east to west coasts truly qualifies as canal, and despite the efforts of its engineer, the acclaimed bridge-builder Thomas Telford, it didn't work first time.

The route was first surveyed in 1733 by another famous Scottish engineer, James Watt, with the aim of sparing coastal shipping and fishing vessels the perilous passage round the north coast of Scotland and through the volatile Pentland Firth. Telford began its construction in 1803, but it was 19 years before it was opened in 1822 – when ships soon discovered that it was too shallow to take their draught. The remedial work took another 25 years. The small capacity of its 29 locks makes the canal virtually useless to modern commercial shipping, which leaves the waterway free to pleasure craft.

In 1952 John Cobb set out to break the world water-speed record on Loch Ness in his speedboat *Crusader*. He had become well-known and well-liked during practice runs in the area, and when his final run ended in disaster, with the boat hitting several large ripples, breaking up and throwing Cobb to his death, a memorial was raised by the local people on the A82, opposite the site of the accident. The austere stone cairn with the Gaelic inscription 'Honour to the brave and the humble' can be seen on the lochside verge 5 km (3 miles) south of Drumnadrochit. Cobb's death incited the feverish theory that the fatal ripples were caused by a disturbed Loch Ness Monster, but more recent analyses of the accident blame a long-running wake from one of his support vessels.

The A82, hacked out of cliffs on the northern shore of the loch, is its main road, and its two waterside junctions at Drumnadrochit and Invermoriston are gateways to the long and lovely glens of Urquhart and Moriston. The old bridge over the River Moriston is another Telford landmark (the new crossing was built after the old structure was undermined by powerful floodwaters in 1951) and nearby is St Columba's Well, which was blessed by the saint and is supposed to have curative powers.

A sidetrip up Glen Moriston is well worth the detour. The glen is conduit to the A887, the road

to Skye. About 21 km (13 miles) from the Invermoriston junction, near the Ceannacroc power station, a cairn marks the site of an episode of Jacobite heroism. In the aftermath of Culloden the glen was refuge to one Roderick Mackenzie, a young Edinburgh lawyer (not all Jacobites were Highlanders) who bore a superficial resemblance to the fugitive Charles Edward Stuart.

Mackenzie's hiding place was discovered by government soldiers who, in the summary manner of 'Butcher' Cumberland's Redcoats, set

Loch Ness, seen here from the south, is Britain's greatest volume of fresh water. Just over 38 km (24 miles) long, it forms part of the chain of lochs and canal which links Scotland's east and west coasts.

about dispatching him. 'Ah, villains!' cried the dying but quick-witted Jacobite. 'You have slain your prince.'

When his head was shown to Cumberland at Fort Augustus the duke sent it to London, where many people swore it was indeed the head of Bonnie Prince Charlie. Mackenzie's brave ruse thus bought the prince time, and for a while the hunt for the Young Pretender was scaled down.

Back on the lochside, the Forestry Commission has long been active and the 'right to roam' policy of Forest Enterprise, who manage their plantations of conifers, has provided a network of forest walks. Among them is a circular route through Allt na Criche Forest which begins 1.6 km (one mile) north of Fort Augustus, takes about an hour to complete and overlooks Cherry Island, the loch's only island which is, in fact, man-made. This crannog, as these ancient artificial islands found in many Scottish lochs are called, was built about 3000 years ago. Their function was to provide defensive refuges and status homesteads for tribal chiefs.

More recent Highland history is given the 'living museum' approach at the nearby Clansman Centre, where a 'Highlander' explains how a local family lived, ate and dressed in the seventeenth century. The centre also exhibits a reconstructed turf house, where a 20-minute tour is available.

At the southern extremity of Loch Ness the A82 continues down the Great Glen to Lochaber, but the attractive crossroads village of Fort Augustus provides a link to the B862, on which road travellers can complete a circuit of the loch by returning to Inverness on a route which eventually follows the banks of the River Ness and Caledonian Canal. Watching boats negotiate the locks at Fort Augustus, where the canal runs through the centre of the village, is a popular spectator sport, but the views up the loch are even more mesmerising.

The village, which had a name-change in the eighteenth century, stands at the crossroads of four of the military roads built by General Wade in the project to control the Highlands after the Jacobite Rebellion of 1715. Its ancient name is Kilcumein, which means Church of Cumein (one of St Columba's successors) but when Wade built a new fort beside the loch he called it Fort Augustus, after the Hanoverian prince William Augustus, Duke of Cumberland.

It was a prescient choice. Cumberland was only a boy at the time, but he notoriously fulfilled his destiny in the region after the second Jacobite Rebellion of 1745 through his brutal treatment of the clans defeated at Culloden. The fort eventually provided the basic structure for an abbey and school of the Benedictine Order, which flourished until very recently for over 120 years. Architecturally Fort Augustus Abbey owes more to military than ecclesiastical design. The greater part of the stronghold's ground floor was incorporated into the abbey buildings, which date from the nineteenth-century East Cloister to a porch added in 1968.

In its southern stages the minor B862 requires careful negotiation – not least for the beguiling distractions of its sinuous route, which includes the viewpoint of Suidhe Chuimein, with fine views across Stratherrick and Strathnairn to the Moray Firth. The road, upgraded, follows the road built by General Wade, the military engineer whose work helped subdue the Highlands after

the '45 by establishing efficient lines of communication between government and garrisons – in this case between Fort Augustus and Fort George, near Inverness.

Just south of the village of Foyers, a fork in the road offers the traveller several options for the journey back to Inverness. The B862, which eventually joins the A9 a few kilometres south of the town, leaves Loch Ness to skirt the shores of modest Loch Mhor, before joining up with the B852 at Dores. Just north of Loch Mhor, the B851 offers an alternative route past a cluster of small lochs and lochans in the valleys of Stratherrick and Upper Strathnairn. This lonely landscape, backed by the desolate moors of the Monadhliath Mountains, is something of a

The locks at Fort Augustus, at the southern extremity of Loch Ness, are a point of negotiation for pleasure craft on the Caledonian Canal, which was opened in 1822.

then the power of the falls has been harnessed (and diminished) by a pump storage plant which feeds electricity into the National Grid. But they are still worth seeing on the nearby forest walk.

The B852 continues through Inverfarigaig Forest, where Dr Samuel Johnson and his biographer James Boswell were entertained in a cottage at An Ire Mhor, taking a dram with an old woman who shared her home with a goat. The good doctor opined that the lochside road 'between birch trees, with the hills above, pleased us much' and at an inn called *The General's Hut* the peripatetic pair dined off 'mutton-chops, a broiled chicken, bacon and eggs and a bottle of Malaga.'

About 16 km (10 miles) from Inverness the road passes through Dores, which is the southern shore's centre for watersports. Its activities are happily restrained; windsurfing and water-skiing are usually only available at weekends. Loch Ness, after all, must take great care not to disturb the peace of its resident behemoth.

The waters near Inverfarigaig (above), have produced the highest number of sightings of the 'monster'.

Loch Ness from the south.

parallel universe to the tourist hotspots and organised leisure of Loch Ness, with opportunities for contemplation, observation and perambulation at Loch Ruthven nature reserve.

The alternative B852 begins to hug the shoreline just after Foyers, where the main spectacle is the Falls of Foyers. The plunge of this 30 m (100 ft) cataract through pinewoods moved the poet Robert Burns to verse and attracted the attention of industrial projects. Until 1968 Foyers was the site of Britain's first aluminium smelter; since

The Loch Ness Monster

It may be hard to spot the Loch Ness Monster, but it's difficult to overlook the Official Loch Ness Exhibition Centre. This impressive, multi-media audit of the evidence (and lack of it) for the presence of an unidentified marine animal in the loch is signalled by the model 'monster' in the gardens of the Drumnadrochit Hotel, a former Victorian fishing hotel.

The exhibition is an honourable attempt to address the questions of both believers and non-believers, and was designed by naturalist Adrian Shine, who runs the Loch Ness Project. Its aim is to be serious in an entertaining way. It invites visitors to assess the facts and theories for themselves by explaining the hoaxes and optical illusions as well as illustrating the scientific facts and reporting the eyewitness accounts – all of which is put in the context of the geology and environment of the loch itself to extend interest beyond the mere sensational.

The first recorded encounter with Nessie in Loch Ness: according to his biographer St Adamnan, St Columba rebuked the Loch Ness Monster as it threatened one of his servants in the 6th century.

Saltwater mammals and fish, including seals and giant sturgeon, have been among the creatures proposed as explanations for the phenomenon of Nessie, which is over 1400 years old. The first recorded sighting came from an impeccable source: St Columba, the great Irish missionary who arrived in Scotland in 563 to establish the mission which turned the little island of Iona into the Christian centre of Europe.

Some years later he set out to convert Brude, king of the Picts, and while on his way to the settlement which became Inverness he asked a servant to swim across the River Ness to fetch a boat. What followed next was documented by his biographer, St Adamnan, a century later.

Suddenly a titanic creature broke the surface of the water 'with a great roar and open mouth', striking terror in the hearts of all but one of the onlookers. St Columba faced down the fish with the sign of the cross and commanded, 'Think not to go further, nor touch thou that man. Quick, go back.'

And it did. It went back into the sunless recesses of the loch and over the next 1400 years its rare appearances were both silent and unthreatening. Stories of a strange beast in Loch Ness next began surfacing in the late nineteenth century (the Nessie syndrome is by no means unique – there have been reports of similar monsters in 265 lakes and rivers throughout the world) but it wasn't until the 1930s, when there were several reported sightings and a controversial snap of the 'monster' was published in a London newspaper, that the popular sport of Nessie-hunting gathered momentum.

In 1933, the *Daily Mail* sponsored the first attempt to track her down, commissioning a big-game hunter and an expert photographer to spend weeks cruising the loch. Their efforts were mischievously rewarded by the hoaxer who printed giant 'spoor' in the lochside mud, using a hippopotamus-foot ashtray, but their mission was to be the first of many which led to the underwater cameras and sonar sweeps which, today, continue to find the evidence inconclusive.

The hunt was inspired by the 'surgeon's photograph' – arguably the most famous of the fuzzy snaps (some of them hoaxes) of the 'monster' which have appeared down the decades. This iconic image was taken by Harley Street consultant and holidaymaker R.K. Wilson, who saw something strange break the surface of the

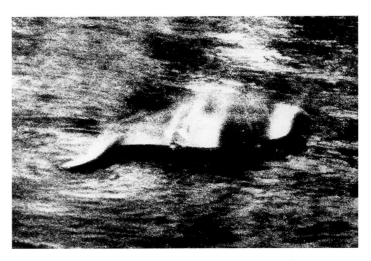

A number of sightings in the 1930s induced a 'monster fever'; such as this mysterious object photographed by Hugh Gray on 12 November, 1933.

An unusual disturbance in Loch Ness, filmed by Malcolm Irving on 12 December, 1933. Monster fever was becoming infectious.

The 'surgeon's photograph': this is possibly the most famous 'snap' of the Loch Ness Monster. It was taken by Robert K. Wilson, a Harley Street consultant on holiday in the Loch Ness area, on 19 April, 1934. The medical man jumped to no conclusions; he merely described his picture as 'a mysterious photo.'

then on. Some were explained by optical illusions on the mirror of the loch – Nessie favours calm, fair conditions for her appearances – and others by overheated imaginations or practical jokes. But there was enough consistently inexplicable evidence to alert the interest of science. And there still is.

Reports by credible eyewitnesses are too numerous to discount. Among the most graphic was given by the late Tim Dinsdale, a dedicated monster-hunter whose film led to the setting up of the Loch Ness Investigation Bureau by the MP David James, Peter Scott and Richard Fitter, which in 1962 became the first scientific project committed to systematic research. As well as shooting a famous cine film of a large, unidentifiable object like a hump moving through the water, Dinsdale and his colleagues recorded seeing a 'telegraph pole-like object moving through the water, protruding at least 10 ft above the surface' from their research craft in Urquhart Bay. This was in 1970.

water near Invermoriston. It appears to show the sinuous neck, small head and heavy shoulders of a large animal. Most alleged sightings of the Loch Ness Monster – with the variation of several humps – have conformed to the profile of this early photograph.

The main road along Loch Ness was upgraded in the 1930s, and the subsequent improved view of the water may explain the relative frequency of sightings from

The telegraph pole (assumed to be the monster's increasingly illustrious neck) surfaced again the following year when Father Gregory, a Benedictine monk from the abbey at Fort Augustus, made one of the most sensational sightings, which was corroborated by a friend. There was 'a terrific commotion in the waters of the bay' and they saw 'quite distinctly the neck of the beast standing out of the water to a height of about 10 feet. It swam towards us at a slight angle, and after about 20 seconds slowly disappeared.'

CASTLE URQUHART LOCH NESS.

THE WINDING ROAD, LOCH NESS.

THE HAUNTS OF THE MONSTER

LOCH NESS AND CASTLE URQUHART.

HALF WAY HOUSE, LOCH NESS.

Early evidence of the infant monster industry – and its tourism potential.
This postcard from the 1930s shows the sinuous road along the north shore which was improved during the 1930s – opening up the loch to more traffic and more sightings.

The prevailing theory around this time favoured the possibility of a colony of prehistoric reptiles living in the loch. The naturalist Sir Peter Scott, one of the founder members of the Loch Ness Investigation Bureau, plumped for the plesiosaur which, with its long neck, short tail and four flippers, has become the model for every Nessie souvenir from soft toy to garden-pond ornament. And their range and variety is ingenious, as a visit to Drumnadrochit demonstrates.

The scientific research continues. Throughout the seventies, eighties and nineties Loch Ness came under the scrutiny of all that modern technology could throw at it: sophisticated underwater photography, observation submersibles, echo sounders, sonar scanners, NASA computers. The Academy of Applied Science in Boston got involved (it still is) and throughout the world scientists teased themselves with sonar images of large objects or mysterious shapes captured by time-lapse

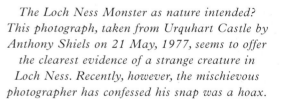

The Loch Ness Monster as nature intended? This photograph, taken from Urquhart Castle by Anthony Shiels on 21 May, 1977, seems to offer the clearest evidence of a strange creature in Loch Ness. Recently, however, the mischievous photographer has confessed his snap was a hoax.

cameras with strobe flashes. Even after 'Operation Deepscan' in 1987, when an armada of 24 motor launches spent a week scouring the loch from side to side and end to end with sonar equipment, the data remained inconclusive. Some of their findings were explained by side echoes from the steep walls of the loch, but at least one echo – from a 'large and moving' object 60 m (200 ft) down – has never been identified.

Loch Ness's geological chronology doesn't fit the plesiosaur theory; this reptile is thought to have become extinct over 70 million years ago, and in any case the experts now believe the waters of Loch Ness are too cold for reptiles. Not everything is yet known about the age of the dinosaurs, however, and it's now believed that some dinosaurs were warm-blooded. What's more, the scientific focus on the loch has exposed some lesser oddities: in 1981 the Loch Ness

Monster hunters: the late Tim Dinsdale (left) was witness to one of the most convincing sightings when he recorded seeing a 'telegraph pole-like object' moving through the water in 1970.
Right: Dan Taylor, another intrepid investigator, in his yellow submarine on Loch Ness. This photograph was taken in 1969.

In the 1980s all that modern technology could offer was brought to bear on the hunt for the Loch Ness Monster. The most ambitious project was Operation Deepscan in October 1987 (left), when a fleet of motor launches equipped with sonar spent a week sweeping the loch from side to side and end to end.

Project came upon a population of Arctic char, who have been secretively living at a depth of 210 m (700 ft) since the last Ice Age over 12,000 years ago.

The Loch Ness Project, whose exhibition at Drumnadrochit regularly updates the hunt for its elusive celebrity, leaves the question open. The seven themed areas of the displays present the evidence with scrupulous detachment, identifying the many japes and misapprehensions which have muddied the waters and leading visitors through the pros and cons while inviting them to make up their own minds. Chief among the pros are the consistency of reliable eye-witness accounts and the ambiguous sonar evidence; chief among the cons is the lack of any viable food supply to sustain a breeding colony of large animals, or even one large animal over many decades.

The legend of the Loch Ness Monster continues on into the 21st century. This view from Urquhart Castle was taken on 30 September, 2000.

Who knows? And what will be gained or lost if we ever find out? Like all mystery monsters, Nessie's greatest allure is her mystery itself. As the naturalist Dr David Bellamy said of the 'something in the loch' in 1991, 'I hope it's there. But I hope they don't find it because if they do, they'll do something nasty to it.'

Inverness – The Capital of the Highlands

The busy tourist hub of Inverness is known as the 'capital of the Highlands' (a title legitimised by the presence of the administrative headquarters of Highland Region, which geographically is Scotland's largest local authority). It has the energetic feel of a small city, with all the familiar infrastructure of transport, commerce and light industry. And as one of the winners in a Millennium competition which sought to confer city status on ambitious towns, Inverness is conscious of its increasingly urban character.

Not every capital deserves its status, but Inverness's claim long predates its modern function of regional HQ. Its strategic position at the northern extremity of the Great Glen – the mighty fault line which slices through the heart of the Highlands – made it a focus of military activity down the centuries, and the opening of the Caledonian Canal in 1822, which created a commercial waterway from east to west coasts, confirmed its future as the most important economic centre north of Aberdeen.

Yet its setting, between two fair firths within a collar of hills, has ready intimations of the Highlands, and its loftier viewpoints – like Tomnahurich, the 66 m (220 ft) high Hill of the Fairies or, some insist, Hill of the Yew Trees – open up vistas of the mountain country in its hinterland. What's more, although relics of its past are not thick on the ground, Inverness and its immediate environs are intimately linked with some of the most potent names and epic events in Scotland's history.

There is no great certainty about the origins of Inverness, although its site at the mouth of the River Ness (which is the meaning of its name) is also the junction of several major routes through the glens, and suggests its earliest function was also that of hub – for military manoeuvres, livestock movements and commercial traffic. Like many settlements of strategic significance it began with a castle – perhaps the Iron Age and Dark Ages earthworks on Craig Phadrig, the 165 m (550 ft) hill 3 km (2 miles) west of the A9, which have been archaeologically sourced to about 500 BC.

The first recorded mention of a castle 'near the Ness' comes from St Adamnan, the seventh-century biographer of St Columba, when he describes the priest's mission in the late sixth century to convert Brude, the pagan king of the Picts. St Adamnan might have been referring to the fort on Craig Phadrig, although historians also offer the option of Auld Castle Hill, known to have been the stronghold of the fatally ambitious nobleman Macbeth in the eleventh century. But it may well have been used defensively for much longer.

When Macbeth seized the crown of Scotland

Inverness's modern urban character belies the ancient history of the city, which has played a key role in many epic events from Scotland's past.

It, too, has long gone, along with its successor. During Scotland's War of Independence against England the town was occupied three times by the English, and when it was finally secured by Robert the Bruce in 1307 he razed the castle to the ground. It rose again, only to become a scene of tragic conflict between Mary Queen of Scots and the rebellious Earl of Huntly, whose family paid grievously for his quarrel with the new young queen. In 1562, when Mary was attempting to consolidate her authority in the northern Highlands, she was refused entry to Inverness Castle by Alexander Gordon, the earl's son. When the castle eventually surrendered he and several other Gordons were hanged (somewhat to the queen's regret and against her better judgement) from its walls.

Inverness was often the centre of clan 'summits', as Scotland's monarchs strove to impose control on the lawlessness of the Highlands. After its troubled castle was twice occupied by Jacobite armies, in 1715 and 1745, it was blown up by the Young Pretender, Charles

This aerial view gives some idea of the complex setting of Inverness, between the Beauly and Moray firths.

by murdering its legitimate owner, Duncan, the killing was avenged by Malcolm Canmore, who destroyed the usurper's castle. Those few details of this chapter in Scottish history which are reliably known were, of course, embellished by Shakespeare, who placed the murder of Duncan in the fortress on Auld Castle Hill. This tainted castle was replaced by a new one, which was built either by Malcolm Canmore in 1057 or David I over 100 years later, when the town became a royal burgh.

Edward Stuart. A year later Bonnie Prince Charlie was back in Inverness, preparing to meet the government army of the Duke of Cumberland, son of George II, which was advancing from Nairn. On 16 April, 1746, the regiments of the Hanoverian king and the clansmen of the Stuart prince came face to face on Culloden Moor, 8 km (5 miles) from the town; and by the end of the day the nature of the Highlands, the future of the Gael and the structure of the clan system had been changed for ever.

After the '45 Inverness Castle languished in ruins until the rubble was cleared in 1834 and the imposing red sandstone building which is now the town's best-known landmark was raised on the site, maintaining a continuity of at least 1000 years. This nineteenth-century castle houses the law courts and local government offices (although it nods at times past in the shape of a statue of the Jacobite heroine Flora Macdonald) and makes a handsome centrepiece to the town, which straddles the River Ness. Nearby, a network of riverside walks and footbridges cross the river by way of Ness Islands to Eden Court Theatre, the cultural heart of the town, and the Victorian cathedral of St Andrew.

Balnain House, also on the left bank, is a restored town house built around 1726 in the early Georgian style. It was used as a hospital for Hanoverian soldiers after the Battle of Culloden, as well as a billet for the Royal Engineers who completed the First Ordnance Survey. Today it

houses the regional office of the National Trust for Scotland and is not open to the public.

The city centre, on the right bank, has no great feeling of antiquity beyond some enduring remnants of its history: the eighteenth-century Tolbooth Steeple which was once the jail, the fifteenth-century bell tower of the High Church, and the fractured pillar of Friars Burying Ground, on the thirteenth-century site of a vanished Dominican priory. The National Trust for Scotland has acquired and restored Abertarff House, which dates from 1592 and was once the urban *pied-à-terre* of the Lovat family, who still supply chiefs to the Clan Fraser and have dwindling estates on the Beauly Firth. The house is distinguished by a rare example of an old stair-

The Kessock Bridge opened in 1982. Linking Inverness with the Black Isle, it carries the A9, the main road north, to Wick and beyond.

Inverness Castle, with its conspicuous site on the River Ness, is the city's most familiar landmark. The present building is 19th century and houses the law courts and local government offices, but it is claimed there has been a castle on this site since the 11th century.

tower and is now the Trust's Highland headquarters.

The tourist authorities make the most of these relics with their 'Inverness Historic Trail'. The Victorian Market, for example, is modern by Scottish standards, as its original name, the 'New Market', suggests. It was built in 1870 and rebuilt after a fire in 1890. Seventeenth-century Dunbar's Hospital was named after Provost Alexander Dunbar, who endowed it as a hospital for the poor and a grammar school. It had a change of use in 1792, when it became a public library, and it now houses flats, a shop and a day centre.

The pedigree of the High Church – the original parish church of Inverness – goes back

much farther. It has held its position on St Michael's Mount since the twelfth century, but apart from the bell tower most of it dates from the 1770s. Jacobite prisoners were held in the church after Culloden, and some of them were executed in the graveyard. And in the local museum, which is near Inverness Castle, is a death mask of Bonnie Prince Charlie.

But perhaps the city's most unusual antiquity is the Clachnacuddin, or Stone of the Tubs, which is now used as a plinth for the restored cross which stands outside the nineteenth-century Town House. Women carrying water from the river once rested their tubs on this homely block, but it has other associations, although none substantiated. Some claim it was a coronation stone. Others insist its destiny is inseparable from that of Inverness, and that if it is ever moved the town's prosperity will suffer; which it certainly shows no sign of doing.

Inverness's road, rail and air links are sophisticated by Highland standards, where the mountainous terrain and convoluted western seaboard make cross-country travel slow. The people of the northern Highlands and islands look to Inverness for all the significant services of a modern town, including hospital treatment, major shopping expeditions and important cultural events; while its airport at Dalcross, which is 13 km (8 miles) north-east of the town, provides swift access to London, Glasgow, and Edinburgh, and maintains vital links with

Scotland's more remote offshore islands.

Nor has Inverness neglected its stake in the leisure industry. Eden Court Theatre and Cinema has a year-round programme of events, and the town supports two other cinemas, including a multiplex.

In Bught Park, in the suburbs near the A82 to Fort William, you will find the Floral Hall, with its fine displays of sub-tropical plants, as well as water features and ornamental gardens. The park is also the epicentre of more physical activity. Here the Aquadome has all the usual thrills of flume engineering, while Inverness Sports Centre, with its wide range of activities, is also a training ground for the local shinty team.

Shinty – a kind of aerial form of hockey similar to Ireland's hurley – is Scotland's oldest game and arguably its most exciting, and the sport is robustly pursued by a network of Highland league teams. But Inverness also has its own football club, Caledonian Thistle, who have recently had some success in the Scottish premier league to which they were promoted in 2004. And, of course, the city is rich in golf courses and well stocked with outlets for outdoor pursuits and resources for exploring its hinterland.

Its site on the River Ness, at the head of the Great Glen, has given Inverness strategic importance over the centuries. Road, rail and air links make it the most accessible city in the Highlands, and the natural capital.

Inverness - The Surrounding Countryside

The Moray Firth from the air, showing the narrows between Chanonry Point on the Black Isle (to the left) and Fort George on its peninsula (to the right).

Although not a peninsular city, Inverness is only minimally landlocked. Six canal locks raise barges and cabin cruisers from the linked series of firths which lie on its doorstep and deposit them on the Caledonian Canal, which then conveys them through Loch Ness, Loch Oich, Loch Lochy and the eight locks of Neptune's Staircase to the west coast seaway of Loch Linnhe. To the north and east there is also water. Firth is the Scottish name

for estuary and Inverness has claims on three of them.

The largest is the Moray Firth, which is the outcome of two smaller estuaries fed by the River Ness and the River Beauly. All three define the southern littoral of an island which isn't an island. The Black Isle is properly a peninsula, a peaceful place of rolling farmland, long strands and coastal flats, and antiquarians still argue about how it got its name. Gaelic scholars suggest that Eilean Dubh, which means black island, may be a corruption of Eilean Dubhthaich, or St Duthus Isle, after an eleventh-century Bishop of Ross; others argue more fancifully that its mild climate keeps it clear of snow when the surrounding countryside is white – and it then looks like a black island.

Whatever the explanation, it is now easily explored from Inverness via the Kessock Bridge, which spans the narrows between the Beauly and Inverness firths, and its modest towns are places of some charm. Fortrose's cathedral has the red sandstone ruins of a church founded by David I for the see of Ross, and Rosemarkie directs walkers beyond its golf course to Chanonry Point, with a stirring view across the firth to Fort George.

According to tradition Scotland's most famous prophet met an ugly death at Chanonry Point. Among other prophecies, the building of the Caledonian Canal was anticipated by the Brahan Seer when he predicted that 'full-rigged ships will be seen sailing at the back of Tomnahurich'. But when he incautiously told the Countess of Seaforth that he could see her absent husband in the arms of a French woman she had him burnt in a barrel of tar.

From the Black Isle it's no great step to the former spa town of Strathpeffer, whose sulphur springs have left it endowed with something of the elegance and prosperity it enjoyed in the

nineteenth century. Its wide street, grand hotels, gardens and pump room (which opened in 1820 and offered 'low-pressure subthermal reclining manipulation douche') will seem familiar to connoisseurs of spa towns, and its low-key Highland setting has even prompted some imaginative commentators to compare it to an Indian hill station.

South of Strathpeffer, across the neck of the Black Isle, the Highland town of Beauly sits on its eponymous river almost at the point where it debouches into the Beauly Firth, and owes its minor celebrity to a long association with the Lovat family, chiefs of the Clan Fraser. A leading Jacobite family in the eighteenth century, the Lovats had the talent to continue producing gifted

Beauly from the air. This little town shares its name with the river and firth, and has a long association with the Lovat family, chiefs of the Clan Fraser.

Frasers well into the twentieth. The sixteenth Lord Lovat founded the heroic Lovat Scouts in 1900. But in recent years their land and fortunes have dwindled, and the family seat, Beaufort Castle, was recently sold.

Beauly is the western outpost of the scatter of pleasant towns within easy reach of Inverness. Although its setting is benign, it sits at the gateway of some of the loneliest and loveliest scenery in Scotland. South-west of the town comely Strathglass, the broad valley of the River Glass, is the conduit to three long and isolated glens, Strathfarrar, Cannich and Affric, which probe deep into the heart of the Northern Highlands. Their single-track roads end in cul-de-sacs, and once you have reached these termini you stand on the edge of a great tract of roadless wilderness.

The hydro-electricity industry is active in all three glens but its impact is discreet and its dams have their own grandeur. The most illustrious is Glen Affric, which begins at the village of Cannich and offers all the classic elements of Highland splendour: gorges and waterfalls, the island-studded loch of Beinn a'Mheadhoin, handsome stands of mixed woodland and the scatter of Caledonian pine trees which, with their rich red boles and dark canopies, are the glen's greatest glory.

The road ends at a car park with close views of some hefty mountains, and at any time of year the parking area holds a clutch of silent, empty cars whose owners seem to have abandoned them. Glen Affric, once the fief of the Clan Chisholm, is the gateway to serious walking country, and the absent car-owners are either climbing the nearby Munros – mountains over 914 m (3000 ft) – or tackling the ambitious, long-distance route through desolate mountain country to the west coast district of Kintail.

Some 65 km (40 miles) south of Inverness lie two more forbidding tracts of wilderness – the Monadhliath Mountains and the high plateau of the Cairngorms – but the hinterland east of the town is very different. The sandy shores of the Moray Firth trim an amiable, civilised landscape of rich farmland, sporting rivers and managed forests, and the firth itself has a population of dolphins (and passing whales) whose presence has opened up a small tourist industry in 'dolphin cruises' operating out of Inverness and North Kessock, on the Black Isle.

The district of Moray and Nairn is also famous for its mild temperatures and sunny climate, while the honey-coloured sandstone of its towns and villages contribute to its fair complexion.

Between Inverness and the seaside town of Nairn the land is pulled into a leafless spit which points towards its opposite number – Chanonry Point – on the Black Isle. On this unlikely spot, near the moribund oil-rig construction yard at Ardersier, is the mightiest artillery fortification in Britain, if not in Europe. Its walls are almost

Glen Affric is the most celebrated, and certainly the most beautiful, of the three long glens which reach deep into the heart of the Northern Highlands from the broad conduit of Strathglass. Its island-studded loch, high mountains and stands of Caledonian pine are the components of a classic Highland glen.

Fort George was built after the Jacobite Rebellion of 1745 to discourage any further dissent in the Highlands and defend the northern territories. It has never seen a shot fired in anger.

1.6 km (1 mile) in circumference and its parade ground alone could be accommodated in the esplanade of Edinburgh Castle. But this prodigious eighteenth-century stronghold is and always has been a white elephant.

Fort George, built after the '45 Jacobite Rebellion to intimidate the Highlands and defend the northern territories of the Hanoverian crown against any further unrest, has never seen a shot fired in anger. It took 21 years to build, it cost nearly £1 billion in today's money and its bastioned defences, batteries of cannon and extensive barracks were designed to be used by government forces of threatening scale. (The magazine could take up to 2500 barrels of gunpowder). But the Jacobite menace was crushed forever at Culloden and the fort survives intact as garrison and regimental museum of the Queen's Own Highlanders.

The historic barracks rooms, open to the public, give some idea of the domestic life of the Scottish soldier down the ages. A model of a private of the 42nd Royal Highlanders sits polishing his musket in the room he shared in 1780 with seven of his comrades, two to a bed. One hundred years later single beds had been introduced for the ranks, while window shutters and fine panelled doors were the privileges of the larger and lighter rooms of officers.

The Battle of Culloden, which took place on 16 April 1746, lasted only 40 minutes, but its impact on the Highlands was devastating. It was the last major battle to be fought on British soil and despite the reckless courage of the clans it was horribly botched by the Jacobite leaders, whose 5000 Highlanders were exhausted, ill-equipped and demoralised by the long retreat from their invasion of England. They were no match for the Duke of Cumberland's 9000 Redcoats and heavy artillery, and their defeat left 1200 dead on the battlefield to the Hanoverians' 76. The slaughter was compounded by 'Butcher' Cumberland's order to hunt down and finish off the wounded, and his soldiers performed this duty so enthusiastically that several bystanders who had come out from Inverness to spectate found themselves on the ends of bayonets.

There's no doubt that the medieval hierarchies and feudal obligations of the clan system were badly in need of reform, but the oppression which followed Culloden and the final rout of Stuart ambitions to recover the British crown almost amounted to cultural genocide.

The wearing of tartan and the kilt and the bearing of arms were proscribed, which also punished the many clans who had either remained neutral or loyal to the government; and the dismantling of the power of the chiefs opened the door, 50 years later, to the abuses of the Clearances, when many of these Highland gentlemen evicted their tenants and sold their land to sheep farmers. From then on, a reluctant Gaelic diaspora was underway, depopulating the Highlands and dispatching the Gael to the

industrial sweatshops of lowland Scotland or the colonies of the British Empire.

Culloden Moor, which lies 8 km (5 miles) east of Inverness, remains a melancholy place – a mass grave where scattered stones mark the Graves of the Clans. The land is now owned by the National Trust for Scotland, who have restored it to something close to its condition in 1746, and their visitor centre makes a credible effort to describe the events and evoke the bedlam of the battle. But it's the site itself with its sad landmarks – the clan gravestones, the Well of the Dead, where wounded Highlanders were cut down again as they drank from a spring – which most poignantly signals the passing of an ancient way of life.

Cumberland's army had advanced from the

Culloden Moor, site of the last battle to be fought on British soil. Here, in 1746, the Jacobite army of Bonnie Prince Charlie was finally crushed by the over-whelming forces of the Duke of Cumberland's Redcoats, and the Stuart dream of recovering their lost crown was ended forever.

coastal town of Nairn, 27 km (17 miles) from Inverness, a place which was long regarded as marking the boundary between Lowlands and Highlands. In the nineteenth century Nairn began to exploit its fine beaches and big blue vistas to the hills on the north side of the Moray Firth and transformed itself into a stylish holiday resort. Today, Nairn still lies at the heart of some colourful attractions and is still a popular golf and tourist resort.

On its doorstep is Cawdor Castle, the fourteenth-century home of the Thane of Cawdor, whose title was one of the prizes promised to Macbeth by the three witches in Shakespeare's play. Chronicles of the eleventh century are obscure and sketchy, and no one knows exactly where Macbeth murdered his king Duncan in order to claim the crown, but the dark deed might have taken place in the original fortress of Cawdor, which was about 1.5 km (a mile) away.

The present structure is an impressive complex of fourteenth, sixteenth- and seventeenth-century buildings, including a central tower, and the interior has a typically eclectic 'stately home' collection of English and Flemish tapestries, domestic and military antiques and handsome works of art, including pictures by the great portrait-painters Romney, Lawrence and Reynolds. Cawdor Castle is open to the public and its gardens and woodland invite visitors to enjoy several nature trails.

Cawdor Castle, near Nairn (above), and seen from the air (opposite), is the 14th-century home of the Thane of Cawdor. The title was one of the prizes promised to the 11th-century Scottish king Macbeth by the three witches in Shakespeare's play. The original fortress was about 1.5 km (a mile) away, and some scholars believe it might have been the scene of Macbeth's murder of Duncan. The present structure is an intriguing complex of 14th, 16th and 17th century buildings which, with their gardens and woodland, are open to the public.

Loch Ness
and Inverness

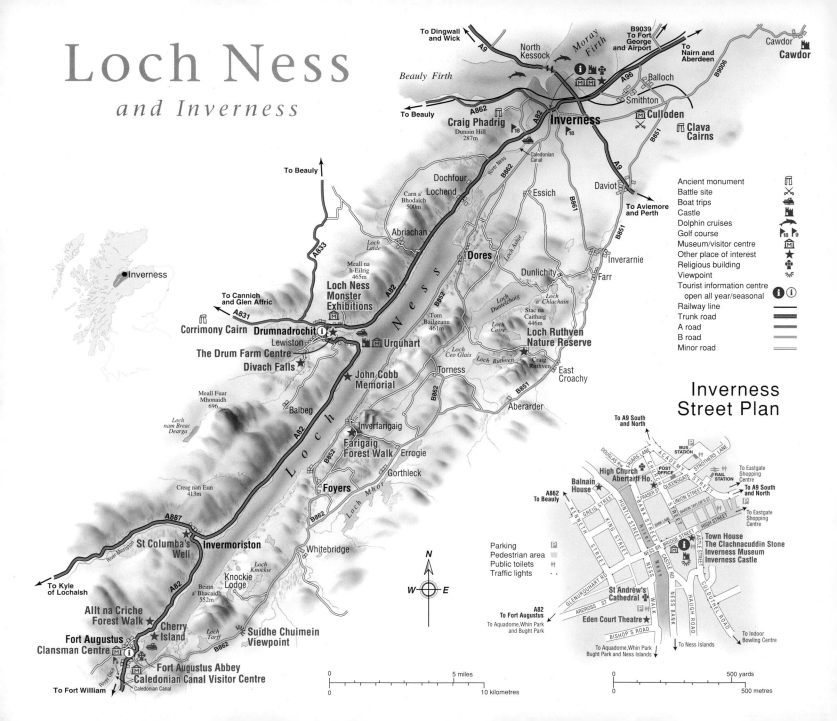

Map labels (Loch Ness region):

To Dingwall and Wick — A9
North Kessock
Moray Firth
B9039 To Fort George and Airport
To Nairn and Aberdeen
Cawdor
Beauly Firth
To Beauly
Inverness
Balloch
Smithton
Culloden
Clava Cairns
A862
Craig Phadrig
Dunain Hill 287m
A96
River Ness
Caledonian Canal
A82
B862
Dochfour
Lochend
Essich
Daviot
To Aviemore and Perth
B861
To Beauly
A833
Carn a' Bhodaich 500m
Abriachan
Loch Laide
Dores
Loch Ashie
Inverarnie
Meall na h-Eilrig 465m
B852
Dunlichity
Farr
Loch Duntelchaig
Loch a' Chlachain
Stac na Caithaig 446m
A831
To Cannich and Glen Affric
Loch Ness Monster Exhibitions
A82
Tom Bailgeann 461m
Loch Ruthven Nature Reserve
Loch Coire
Loch Ruthven
Craig Ruthven
Corrimony Cairn
Drumnadrochit
Lewiston
Urquhart
Loch Ceo Glais
Torness
East Croachy
The Drum Farm Centre
Divach Falls
John Cobb Memorial
Meall Fuar Mhonaidh 696
Balbeg
Loch
Ness
B852
B851
Aberarder
Inverfarigaig
Loch nam Breac Dearga
Farigaig Forest Walk
Errogie
B862
Gorthleck
Creag nan Eun 413m
Foyers
Loch Mhor
A887
Whitebridge
St Columba's Well
Invermoriston
River Moriston
Loch Knockie
Knockie Lodge
To Kyle of Lochalsh
A82
Beinn a' Bhacaidh 552m
Allt na Criche Forest Walk
Cherry Island
Loch Tarff
Suidhe Chuimein Viewpoint
Fort Augustus
Clansman Centre
B862
Fort Augustus Abbey
Caledonian Canal Visitor Centre
To Fort William
River Oich
Caledonian Canal

N W—E S (compass)

Legend:

Ancient monument
Battle site
Boat trips
Castle
Dolphin cruises
Golf course
Museum/visitor centre
Other place of interest
Religious building
Viewpoint
Tourist information centre
  open all year/seasonal
Railway line
Trunk road
A road
B road
Minor road

Scale bars:
0 — 5 miles
0 — 10 kilometres

Inverness Street Plan

To A9 South and North
DOUGLAS RW
FRIARS LANE
ACADEMY ST
BUS STATION
STROTHERS LANE
RAIL STATION
To Eastgate Shopping Centre
To A9 South and North
To Eastgate Shopping Centre
High Church
Abertarff Ho.
POST OFFICE
CHURCH ST
QUEENSGATE
UNION ST
A862
To Beauly
Balnain House
GREIG STREET
KING STREET
HUNTLY STREET
FRASER ST
BANK STREET
BANK LANE
BARON TAYLOR'S ST
BRIDGE STREET
CASTLE STREET
High Street
Town House
The Clachnacuddin Stone
Inverness Museum
Inverness Castle
KENNETH STREET
NESS BR
NESS ST
CASTLE RD
CULDUTHEL ROAD
GLENURQUHART RD
ARDROSS ST
St Andrew's Cathedral
NESS WALK
NESS BANK
HAUGH ROAD
A82
To Fort Augustus
To Aquadome, Whin Park and Bught Park
Eden Court Theatre
BISHOP'S ROAD
To Aquadome, Whin Park, Bught Park and Ness Islands
To Ness Islands
To Indoor Bowling Centre

Inverness Street Plan Legend:
Parking
Pedestrian area
Public toilets
Traffic lights

Scale bars:
0 — 500 yards
0 — 500 metres

Inverness (inset Scotland map)